Author Bio:

Dale Walters

Highlights from Dale's Amateur Career:

- Olympic Bronze Medal 1984 Los Angeles
- 5-Time Canadian Champion
- Selected Outstanding Boxer in Canada at 3 National
    Championships
- Pan-American Games 1983 Venezuela
- Commonwealth Games 1983 Australia
- Defeated World Champ Slavimer Zabart 1982 Germany
- Defeated #2 World Ranked Todd Hickman 1984 Edmonton
- Stockholm Open Gold Medal 1984 Sweden
- Defeated U.S. National Champion Lyndon Walker 1984
    Florida
- B.C. and Alberta Golden Gloves Champion

Dale can be contacted at:

    www.ringsidefitness.com
    or by email at:
    dwringside@shaw.ca

The Great Speed Bag Handbook

WRITTEN BY:
Dale Walters

RESEARCHED BY:
Michael Jespersen

EDITED BY:
EXPERT: STRETCHING & GENERAL FITNESS
Andre Noel Potvin, M.SC., C.S.C.S., CES

GENERAL EDITOR
Michael Jespersen

COPY EDITOR
Amanda Vogel

First Printing

Published December 2004
Productive Fitness Products Inc.
2289-135A St.
Surrey, B.C. V4A 9V2

For quantity discounts please call toll free:
1-800-994-9097
or write:
Productive Fitness Publishing Inc.
#102 - 1645 Jill's Court,
Bellingham, WA 98226
or e-mail
  info@productivefitness.com

Visit our Web site: www.productivefitness.com

Walters, Dale, 1963-
    The great speed bag handbook / Dale Walters, Andre Noel Potvin

ISBN 0-9731262-3-X

    1. Bag punching. I. Potvin, André Noël, 1961- II. Title

GV1137.6.W343 2004   796.83
C2004-906486-X

TABLE OF
CONTENTS

Speed Bag Exercises

INTRODUCTION

Agility, speed, balance, reaction time and hand-eye coordination are some of the most important skills necessary for survival in the boxing ring. One of the best tools to help a boxer develop these skills is the speed bag. Most, if not every, notable boxer is very proficient at working the speed bag. However, you don't have to be a boxer to benefit from using the speed bag. A non-boxer can realize all the same benefits—and get a great workout at the same time.

Learning how to hit a speed bag without guidance can be extremely difficult and frustrating. This handbook was created for beginners to speed bag training. You will learn how to master the basic punches, increase the frequency of your hits and progress to combination punches. The simplest and best way to learn the speed bag is to master each step before continuing to the next level. Start slowly—and practice, practice, practice.

Once you master the basics of hitting the bag, you can get a challenging cardio workout. As you become comfortable with hitting the bag consecutively, you can begin to incorporate body movement and more intensity into your routine. For example, moving from left to right or ducking and punching increases heart rate and makes you sweat.

Keep in mind that the speed bag moves with predictability and certainty only if the person hitting it uses precise and certain movements. As you learn to hit the bag with rhythm, timing and balance, you'll begin to experience the fun and stress relief of speed bag training.

Success comes with practice. Good Luck.

Note: If you are right handed you lead with your left side (left hand and foot). This is called the orthodox stance and the way the majority of the population would stand. If you are left handed you lead with your right side (right hand and foot). This is called a southpaw stance. We have tried to show both perspectives wherever possible.

GENERAL GUIDELINES
& SAFETY

- Follow the manufacturer's instructions for installation and safety.
- Use hand wraps or gloves when hitting the speed bag.
- Warm up your arms and shoulders with light stretching and push-ups before hitting the bag.
- Set the speed bag at the correct height to avoid straining or accidentally hitting the rebound board.
- Keep the floor clear of debris.
- A sturdy, well-secured and thick rebound board is best for getting a good bounce.
- Always wear proper footwear; running shoes are ideal.
- Wear light, nonrestrictive clothing that allows you to move freely.
- Avoid locking your elbows when hitting or locking your knees while standing. Maintain a slight bend in both knees and both elbows.
- Remove all jewelry, especially rings, before hitting the speed bag.
- Make sure no one is standing near the bag while you are hitting it.
- When mounting the speed bag to a wall, check that the rebound board is level.
- Before each workout, ensure that the speed bag is secure and no parts have loosened.
- Never hang from the rebound board.
- Stop training if you feel any pain.

SPEED
BAGS

Like any sports equipment, a good speed bag should last several years, depending on how frequently it is used. Eventually, however, the leather covering will wear thin and the bag's "bladder" will come through.

Size

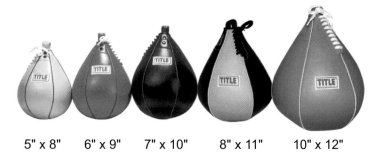

5" x 8"   6" x 9"   7" x 10"   8" x 11"   10" x 12"

Generally, large bags help you work on your power, while small bags are designed for improving hand speed. The best bag to learn on is a mid sized bag because it is easier to regulate speed and maintain control. Speed bags are measured in diameter and height. Specific bag sizes vary according to the manufacturer; most bags range in size from 5" x 8" to 10" x 12".

Proper Inflation

How hard should a speed bag be blown up? The bag's hardness is a matter of personal choice, as long as you don't over-inflate it. Keep in mind that the amount of air in the bag affects its speed; the harder the bag, the faster it moves.

Using a hand pump, inflate the speed bag until it is smooth and wrinkle-free. Then squeeze the bag by pressing your thumbs into the sides. The bag should be firm, with a little give. Next, hit the bag to see if it feels comfortable.

If it feels too hard, release some air. Once it feels good and is rebounding well, you are ready to go.

Deflation

To deflate the bag, insert just the air pump's needle into the bag's bladder, allowing the air to slowly escape.

Bladders

The bag's bladder is made of a rubber or plastic material that is not as strong as the leather covering that protects it. Therefore, you may have to replace the bladder before the leather covering. The biggest reason for bladders malfunctioning is over-filling them with air. The bag should be firm, but not rock-hard. A second reason is simply the pounding they take. Bladders come in the same sizes as the leather covers.

To replace a bladder, loosen the laces at the top of the cover. Deflate the bladder completely, then remove it from inside the leather cover. When putting in the new bladder, make sure to insert the air valve stem into the hole at the bottom of the speed bag cover. Use an ordinary hand pump and needle to inflate the bladder.

Latex Rubber

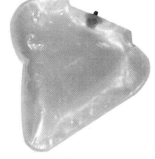
Plastic

Most bladders are either rubber or plastic. Rubber is longer lasting and a litter heavier than plastic which is lighter and faster but not as durable.

SETTING UP A
SPEED BAG

Deciding on the type of speed bag unit to set-up and finding the ideal spot are the first two decisions you'll need to make.

You may choose to have a speed bag permanently mounted on a wall or have a freestanding unit. If you are wall mounting, the unit can either be fixed or adjustable height.

If only one person, or even several people of the same height, are using the same bag then a fixed structure is fine. If several people of varying heights are using the bag then an adjustable unit is better. It is important for the speed bag to be set at the right height. After the speed bag platform and bag are installed, the bag should be level with your eye-line (see pg. 10).

Wall-mount fixed

Whether you have a fixed or adjustable unit it must be securely attached to the wall studs. Some walls may even require reinforcing for added support. Even though the speed bag is small in comparison to heavy bags, the rebound board takes a tremendous amount of pounding; therefore, it needs a

Wall-mount adjustable

great deal of support to help the bag flow smoothly.

Note that some bags are easier than others to adjust.

Free standing units are ideal for people that have nowhere to hang a bag but have enough space to set one up. Free standing units come in a variety of different types. Some are only for heavy bags while others are designed to accommodate heavy bags, speed bags and reflex bags. These units are never as sturdy as mounting a bag

Free standing

from the wall. As well, these units limit how far you can move around the bag.

Swivels

The swivel attaches the speed bag to the rebound board. There are two parts to the swivel. The base of the swivel screws into the center of the rebound board. There is also a ball bearing that screws into the base. Swivels attach to the speed bag with either an S-hook or a link hook.

S-hook swivel

The S-hook and the link hook do pretty much the same job. It is difficult to tell any difference between the two when you hit the bag. However, it is much easier to change the bag with an S-hook. The link style requires needle-nose pliers to change the bag. If you are worried about theft, you can easily slip the bag off the S-hook and leave the base screwed into the rebound board. With the link style, however, you need vise grips to unscrew the swivel's base before you can take the bag with you.

Link hook swivel

Rebound Board

Rebound boards vary in diameter and thickness. Most range from 3⁄4" to 2" thick and 24" to 30" in diameter. The thicker the board, the less vibration. Make sure the rebound board is big enough to allow larger speed bags to bounce without touching the edge of the board. The swivel base is screwed into the center of the rebound board. The base is threaded to allow the swivel to be screwed in. (not all swivels can be screwed into the same base). The loop at the top of the speed bag attaches to the swivel.

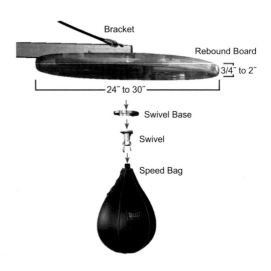

Proper Height

Your eyes should be at the same level as the belly of the bag. You should be able to stand flat-footed when performing speed bag strikes.

Proper Height Adjustment

ACCESSORIES

Handwraps

There are two basic types of hand wraps: stretchy and non-stretchy. Some people prefer the feel of the stretchy hand wraps against their knuckles. Others like the fact that the non-stretchy variety allows you to easily monitor the wrap's tightness.

Hand wraps come in different lengths. Some are as short as eight feet and others as long as 18 feet. The length of your wrap depends on the size of your hands (small, medium or large). You may also like more protection around your hands, which affects the length of the wrap you choose.

Most training hand wraps come with thumb loops. Slipping your thumbs into these loops helps you start wrapping your hands. Hand wraps should also have Velcro straps to secure the completed wrap in place.

Gloves

Many people prefer not to wear gloves when they hit the speed bag. Others like the protection and feel of gloves.

Unless you have very tender hands, you do not need to wear heavy-duty bag gloves when hitting a speed bag. In fact, bigger gloves tend to get in the way when you hit the speed bag.

Weight training gloves are an alternative to hand wraps and bag gloves.

STANCE AND BODY
MOVEMENT

Normal Boxer's Stance
Foot positioning

Choose a hand to jab or lead with and place the same-side foot slightly in front of the other when you hit the bag. Your foot position should stay the same until you become more proficient at hitting the bag. As you improve, you will feel more confident about being lighter on your feet and moving your feet as you hit.

Foot Position

Body movement

Your level of proficiency when hitting the speed bag determines your degree of body movement. Your arm movements determine the bag's direction. And the hand striking the bag determines where to distribute your weight. For example, when striking the bag with your left hand, your weight is mostly on your left leg. When striking the bag with your right hand, your weight is mostly on your right leg. As you begin to transfer your weight and shift your balance from side to side, your shoulders will sway side to side, as well. At this point, you will feel your whole body involved in each punch. You should feel the rhythm of your punches coming from the soles of your feet. Your weight and balance change rhythmically and your punches flow like music.

Most boxers want to be light on their feet, hitting the speed bag while on the balls of their feet. Others dance on their toes or simply stand stationary. No matter what stance you choose, your fists and arms will always be moving and your whole body will be involved in throwing punches. A speed bag always allows you to have your own individual expression and movements.

Orthodox fighter's stance

Your feet are about shoulder width apart with your left foot in front and your right foot behind and slightly off to the side. Your hips, torso and shoulders should be at a 45% angle to the bag.

Orthodox

Southpaw fighter's stance

Your feet are about shoulder width apart with your right foot in front and your left foot behind and slightly off to the side. Your hips, torso and shoulders should be at a 45% angle to the bag.

Southpaw

HOW TO HIT THE
BAG

Hand points of contact

The main points of contact with the speed bag are your fists. The two areas on the fists are the outside of the fist and the front of the fist. There are no written rules on exactly how you must hit the bag so you can develop a lot of your own style and technique. While it is important to develop the basic hitting skills once you are comfortable with the bag you can be as artistic and inventive as you like.

Outside of fist

The first point of contact to learn is the outside of your fist, or the opposite side of your fist from your thumb. Keep your fist loosely clenched until you strike then tighten it somewhat and after the strike loosen it again. This will be the most used point of contact.

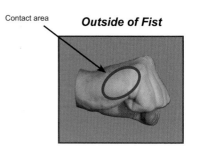

Contact area **Outside of Fist**

Front of fist

The second point of contact is the knuckle portion of your fist. Focus on using the center two knuckles as the main point of contact with the speed bag. Keep your fist loosely clenched until you strike then tighten it somewhat and after the strike loosen it again.

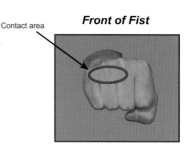

Contact area **Front of Fist**

When you learn how to combine both these points of contact, you will look like a champion boxer and can begin incorporating other body parts. Many boxers only use the two points of contact with their fists, but others throw in elbows or even the forehead for fun.

Bag Point of contact

The speed bag is connected to a swivel so it is always moving. Hit the middle of the bag at the most expanded part. As you face the bag, hit its front and sides.

Left Side Strike Area   Right Side Strike Area

Front Forward/Cross/Jab Strike Area

Front Forward Strike

Jab

Cross

Side Strike

TIMING

Timing involves consistently selecting the precise moment to hit the bag on its rebound and in an optimal position to minimize effort and maximize output. Timing is influenced by the amount of power you use when making contact with the bag. The harder you hit, the faster the bag will go. Therefore, when learning how to hit a speed bag, do not hit it too hard; it is easier to learn by hitting the bag softly and smoothly. Controlling the power with which you hit the bag is the first step to becoming more proficient.

Mastering timing

When starting out, use the hand that feels most comfortable. Hit the bag directly forward with the outside of your fist. Follow through with your hit and bring your fist back to the start position. When you hit the bag, count the rebounds out loud or in your head.

The first time the bag hits the rebound board going forward, count one. When it hits the rebound board coming back, count two. As the bag hits the rebound board going forward again, count three. And when it hits the board coming back, count four.

The bag will have slowed down as it goes forward one more time. The count at this point is five. Get ready to strike the bag again as it comes toward you. Once the bag has made five rebounds, hit it again in the same direction, with the same hand and with the same amount of power as your last hit.

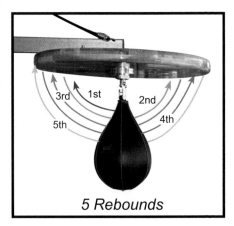

5 Rebounds

Beginner or Power Cross

Continue this exercise until you master it. Then, repeat the above steps with your other hand until you feel comfortable moving to the next step. Do not rush this process. Timing is a basic technique you must know for hitting a speed bag.

The next step involves hitting the bag with both hands, one after the other. Start with your best hand. After counting five rebounds, use your other hand, immediately hitting the bag again. Continue this exercise for as long as you can, or until you feel comfortable progressing to the step described below.

Now hit the bag faster by taking away one of the revolutions. Instead of counting to five, strike the bag after count three. Once again start with your best hand, moving to your other hand and then combining the two. Do everything slowly. Be patient.

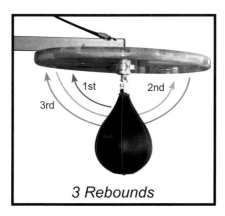

3 Rebounds

Advanced

Trying to hit the bag on the rebound by watching and waiting for the right moment to strike is almost impossible. Listening for the rebounds and mentally counting them before you strike are the only ways to perfect your timing.

RHYTHM

Rhythm is the flow or recurring pattern of the speed bag hitting the rebound board. Timing and rhythm go hand in hand. However, when we talk about timing, the focus is on the arms and fists. Rhythm on the other hand, involves movement of the whole body. You can not improve your rhythm if you only use your arms to hit. When throwing punches at an opponent in the ring, the punch literally starts from the bottom of your feet. You transfer your weight to get punching power. While learning to hit a speed bag, hit it fast, not hard. The better you get, the shorter and crisper your punches will become. This is what varies the speed and rhythm of the bag.

When punching an opponent in the ring, you want to be on the balls of your feet. Assume the same stance for hitting the speed bag to be mobile and rhythmic. Learn to play with rhythm by changing the timing and the number of rebounds. You will notice that the sound of the bag hitting the rebound board creates a rhythm. The rhythm is not much different than the sound of hands banging out a beat on bongo drums. The direction you hit the bag and the power with which you hit it will also determine rhythm. The speed bag

Bongo drums

allows for individual expression as you control the rhythm and sounds that vibrate through the gym or training room.

BALANCE

In order to have timing and rhythm, you must have balance, or physical equilibrium. Balance is the ability to remain upright and in control, whether you are stationary or in motion. Kicking a ball, taking a slap shot or throwing a punch all require balance. Whenever you use both hands to punch, you must transfer your weight from side to side. This means that your ability to balance is challenged on each side, as well. If you only hit the bag with your left hand, your balance will be predominantly on your left side. Likewise, if you only hit the bag with your right hand, your balance will be predominantly on your right side. When starting out, balance on one side first, then practice balancing on the other side. Get comfortable with your balance on both sides before transferring your weight from side to side. Once you can do this with the bag flowing evenly, you can begin to change the rhythm to test your balance.

Boxer's stance

The boxer's stance is an optimal position for maintaining balance while being able to move quickly in any direction. Having your feet at shoulder width apart gives a good base of support. If your feet are spaced too wide or too narrow your balance is compromised. With your knees bent you will be able to react quickly.

HOW TO WRAP
YOUR HANDS

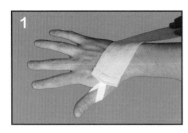

Spread fingers apart, palm down; use thumb loop.

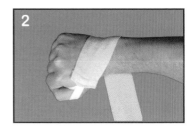

Make a fist; keep wrist straight.

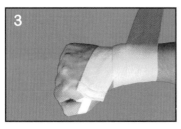

Three loops around wrist, snug but not tight. Gradually wrap towards forearm, 1/2 the width of wrap on existing wrap.

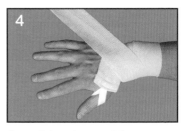

Open fist and spread fingers wide. Pull wrap up toward little knuckle.

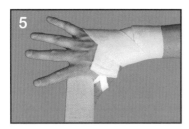

Keep fingers spread apart as you bring wrap under palm.

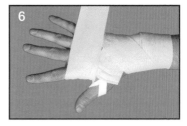

Continue spreading your fingers, looping the wrap over and under the knuckles twice.

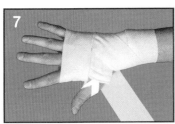

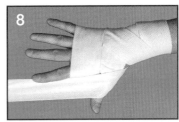

Bring the wrap from the base of the little finger toward the base of the thumb.

Pull wrap over the top of thumb.

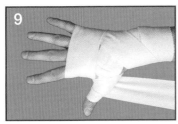

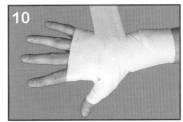

Pull wrap under the thumb as smoothly as possible.

Take the wrap back over the top of the wrist and over the little knuckle.

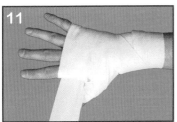

Bring wrap from under the hand over index (big) knuckle and then angle toward wrist.

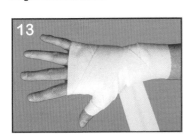

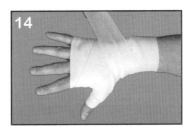

Do a complete loop around wrist then bring up toward little knuckle.

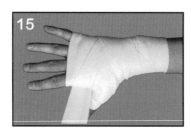

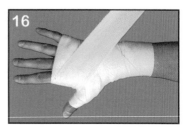

Pull the strap under the palm, feeding it between index finger and thumb.

Pull over the top of the hand, toward wrist.

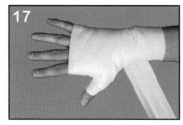

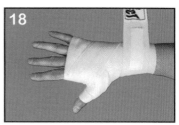

Finish by doing a full circle around wrist.

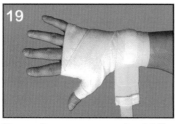

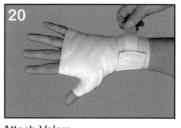

Do another wrap around wrist if you have enough strap.

Attach Velcro.

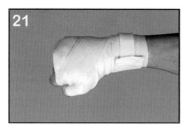

Make a fist.

STRETCHING

BY ANDRE NOEL POTVIN, MSc, CSCS, CES

Why Stretch?

Regular stretching helps maintain and improve flexibility. The definition of flexibility is a joint's ability to move through a normal range of motion (ROM). Each joint has its own degree of flexibility; therefore, it's possible to be very flexible in one joint and stiff in another. The primary limitation in joint ROM is due to the tough connective tissue running through the muscle belly. Other factors that influence flexibility include:

- age
- genetics
- activity (previous exercise experience)
- joint structure (injury or no injury)
- gender (women are generally more flexible than men)
- body temperature (slightly warmer than normal is more effective)
- opposing muscle tightness (opposing muscles are responsible for returning limbs to their original position).

Stretching is the practice of tissue elongation, or lengthening muscle and connective tissue for the purpose of reducing tension around a specific joint. Stretching allows the joint to move more freely. Some benefits of stretching include:

- increased joint range of motion
- reduced joint stress due to muscular imbalances
- reduced chronic soft-tissue pain (i.e., neck, back, knees, etc.)
- increased relaxation
- enhanced well-being

When stretching, keep the following points in mind.

- Stretch to a mild-intensity (30%-40% of maximum intensity). The stretch should feel like a comfortable pull.
- Hold stretches for 30-60 seconds, until the muscle relaxes. When you begin a stretch, your muscles will feel tight; this feeling subsides as the muscle relaxes, then elongates.
- Stretch when your muscles are warm, ideally after physical activity, such as resistance training or aerobics. Stretching with warm muscles enhances results. Avoid stretching cold muscles.
- Pay extra attention to your tightest joints. Flexibility is joint-specific; focus on all joints with restricted ROM.
- Proper body alignment is critical for getting maximum results. Carefully study and follow the stretch positions and explanations in this handbook.
- Repeat each stretch 2-3 times.
- Breathe deeply as you stretch; this enhances relaxation by stimulating the Central Nervous System (CNS).

IMPORTANT SAFETY TIPS

- STOP stretching if you feel pain.
- NEVER push against or force a joint beyond its limit.
- NEVER hold a stretch longer than 90 seconds. Doing so could weaken the tissue and increase the risk of injury and/or irritation.
- If you feel pain during any of these stretches, STOP IMMEDIATELY and see your physician.

Flexibility Training Guidelines

Intensity	• Using a scale of 1-10, stretch at about a 3-4 intensity level (1=very mild stretch, and 10=extreme stretch). You should feel a comfortable pulling sensation, never pain.
	1 out of 10=very very mild
	10 out of 10=extremely intense
Time	• Hold each stretch for 30-60 seconds. • Perform each stretch 2-3 times.
Other Variables	• For optimal results, stretch after a warm-up or aerobic activity when the muscles are warm.

Stretch Routine

① Neck Retractions/Chin Tucks
(Stretches: neck extensors)

- In a standing position, poke your chin and head forward, then draw your chin backward, flattening the back of your neck.
- Keeping neck retracted (chin in), tuck chin down, toward your chest.
- Hold for 30-60 seconds; repeat 2-3 times. Repeat often during the day.

② Head Tilts
(Stretches: scalenes, upper trapezius)

- Tilt head to the right and lower your left shoulder.
- Place right hand on left side of head to gently intensify stretch.
- Hold for 30-60 seconds; repeat 2-3 times. Switch sides.
- Caution: Be very gentle when intensifying this stretch.

(3) Head Turn
(Stretches: neck rotators)

- Place right index and middle finger on left side of jaw.
- Place left hand on back of head, on the right side.
- Gently rotate head to the right, using hands to intensify stretch.
- Hold for 30-60 seconds; repeat 2-3 times. Switch sides.

(4) Ball Arch
(Stretches: chest, ribs, shoulders, abs, spine)

- Lie face-up on a stability ball.
- Place hands behind head, holding abs tight.
- Squeeze shoulder blades together, opening elbows to the side.
- Arch your back over the ball with feet flat on floor, keeping neck neutral as you slightly look up toward ceiling.
- Breathe deeply, expanding the chest.
- Start by holding for 5 seconds, then releasing. Gradually increase over time to hold for 30-60 seconds; repeat 2-3 times.

(5) Handcuff Towel
(Stretches: anterior deltoid, chest, biceps)

- Hold a towel behind your back with palms facing body.
- Squeeze shoulder blades together and pull arms backward.
- Keep abs tight and don't arch lower back.
- Hold for 30-60 seconds; repeat 2-3 times.

Note: Avoid leaning forward, rolling shoulders forward or poking your neck forward.

Advanced: Grip fingers together and repeat as above without the towel.

(6) Overhead Reach
(Stretches: latissimus dorsi)

- Standing or kneeling, interlace fingers and reach arms overhead, palms down.
- Keep neck neutral; avoid poking head forward.
- Hold for 30-60 seconds; repeat 2-3 times.

Variation: Clasp the left wrist, pulling arm up and to the right. Repeat on left.

Variation

Seated Arm Cross-Over Hug
(Stretches: rhomboids, middle and lower trapezius, erector spinae)

- Sit with legs slightly bent in front of you.
- Cross arms, keeping them straight; hold right thigh with left hand and left thigh with right hand.
- Sit back, using your abs.
- Hold for 30-60 seconds; repeat 2-3 times.

Shoulder Towel Stretch
(Bottom arm stretch– external rotators, anterior deltoid)
(Top arm stretch - posterior deltoid, triceps)

- Hold one end of towel in right hand, raising right arm overhead.
- With towel hanging behind back, grab other end with left hand.
- Pull up on towel with right hand, straightening arm, to stretch left (bottom) shoulder.
- Pull down on towel with left hand, straightening arm, to stretch right (top) shoulder.
- Hold for 30-60 seconds; repeat 2-3 times. Switch sides.

Note: Keep shoulder blades squeezed together.

Bottom arm stretch   Top arm stretch

Single-Knee Corkscrew
(Stretches: gluteus maximus, obliques, erector spinae, piriformis)

- Sit with left leg straight and right leg bent, knee close to chest and right foot on opposite side of left knee.
- Place right hand on floor behind you for support.
- Wrap left arm around right knee, pulling up into left shoulder.
- Rotate torso until you feel a comfortable stretch.
- Breathe deeply. As you exhale, twist a little more.
- Hold for 30-60 seconds; repeat 2-3 times. Switch sides.

Note: This stretch works best when you sit up as straight as possible.

Runner's Hip Stretch
(Stretches: tensor fasciae latae, iliopsoas, rectus femoris, obliques, erector spinae, spine)

- Take a large step forward with right leg.
- Place a stability ball under right buttock for support, keeping most of your weight on legs.
- Bend left knee down and toward front leg.
- Twist torso to the right, placing right hand on ball (or right buttock), and left hand on right side of right thigh.
- Squeeze buttocks and tilt pelvis forward. (Imagine pelvis is a bucket tilting to pour water behind you.)
- You should feel the stretch in the left hip and thigh.

Hold for 30-60 seconds; repeat 2-3 times. Switch sides.

Note: Avoid arching lower back

Advanced: Cross left foot behind you and to the right; repeat as above.

Variation

Seated Towel Stretch
(Stretches: hamstrings, gastrocnemius)

- Sit with both legs slightly bent in front of you.
- Wrap a towel or rope around left foot.
- Gently straighten left leg until you feel a comfortable stretch.
- Pull left toes and foot toward you.

Hold for 30-60 seconds; repeat 2-3 times. Switch sides.

Note: Lift chest and straighten back by arching through lower back; retract shoulder blades (avoid rounding them forward) and keep neck neutral, or look slightly down.

Bent-Knee Stretch
(Stretches: quadriceps, hip flexors)

- Hold left ankle while standing.
- Pull left heel to buttocks, or until you reach a comfortable stretch.
- Point left knee toward floor.
- Tilt pelvis. (Imagine pelvis is a bucket tilting to pour water behind you.)
- Keep spine straight and upright, chest lifted and head neutral.

Hold for 30-60 seconds; repeat 2-3 times. Switch sides.

Modification: For a stiff knee or quadriceps, place left foot on a bench or chair.

Variation

Cross-Leg Stretch
(Stretches: gluteus medius and minimus)

- Sit on a chair or bench and cross left leg so left ankle rests on right knee.
- Sit straight with chest lifted and shoulder blades slightly squeezed together.
- Gently press on left knee with left hand until you feel a comfortable stretch.
- Hold for 30-60 seconds; repeat 2-3 times. Switch sides.

Inner Thigh Stretch
(Stretches: adductors)

- Stand with feet wide apart, both hands on left thigh.
- Perform a slight squat, leading with buttocks and keeping chest lifted.
- Shift your weight to the left until you feel a comfortable stretch.
- Angle left foot a little toward the left, with left knee aligned over second toe.
- Point right foot forward, keeping sole flat on floor.
- Hold for 30-60 seconds; repeat 2-3 times. Switch sides.

Bent-Knee Calf Stretch
(Stretches: soleus)

- Step forward with right foot, placing right heel on floor, toes up and both hands on left thigh.
- Slowly squat with left leg until you feel a comfortable stretch in left calf. Keep left heel on floor.
- Pull left toes toward your shin to intensify.
- Hold for 30-60 seconds; repeat 2-3 times. Switch sides.

Note: Keep heels down and weight on back leg; lift chest and slightly arch lower back.

Straight-knee Calf Stretch
(Stretches: gastrocnemius)

- Step forward with right foot.
- Straighten left leg, gradually pressing left heel to floor.
- Stop when you feel a comfortable stretch in left calf.
- To intensify, pull left toes toward shin.
- Hold for 30-60 seconds; repeat 2-3 times. Switch sides.

Note: Keep your heels down and weight on back leg; lift chest and slightly arch lower back.

Basic
PUNCHES

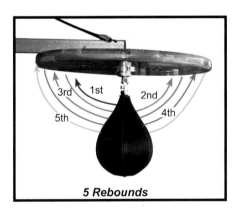

5 Rebounds

Five rebounds

The secret to learning the speed bag is to hit it softly and smoothly at first. Count the revolutions as the bag hits the rebound board. After you hear the fifth hit, the bag will be coming toward you.

For Fitness: Remember to do all of the exercises on the opposite side as well. Instead of leading with your left side you lead with your right. You then reverse the sides and direction.

Basic Punches

Front Forward Strike

Front Forward Strike:
5 Rebounds

1. Start with your left hand. Make a fist and raise it to your eye-line with your elbow at about shoulder level. With your thumb toward you and your wrist straight, prepare to strike the bag with the outside of your fist.

①

②

2. Strike the bag in the center so it travels straight back and rebounds forward in a straight line. Immediately bring your hand back to the start position.

3. Let the bag hit the board five times, counting each hit as it happens. When the bag has rebounded five times, strike it again with the same hand; use the same amount of power and hit it in the same direction. Each time the bag has rebounded five times, strike it again.

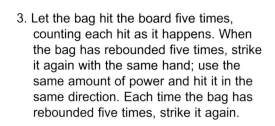

③

Note: Hit the bag directly forward with an even amount of power and count in your head the number of times that it rebounds off the rebound board.

Front Forward Strike

1 & 2. Repeat the same steps as on page 30, but use your right hand this time.

3. When you feel comfortable using both your right and left hands, progress to using both hands consecutively.

Southpaw Front Forward Strike

Using the southpaw stance for the front forward strike does not make a big difference, but it is useful for adding variety.

Basic Punches

Basic Punches

**Front Forward Strike
(both hands)**

Front Forward Strike:
5 Rebounds

1 to 3. This sequence of front forward strikes is a combination
of the left and right hands. Strike the bag with your left hand.
After letting the bag rebound five times, hit it with your right
hand. Shift your body weight from side to side.

4 to 6. Again, let the bag rebound five times, shifting your weight
from one side to the other. Continue until you get tired or
bored.

Boxer's Box
The front forward strike is not a punch that you would use in
the ring. It is strictly used on the speed bag to improve
hand/eye coordination and timing.

Jab

Jab: 5 Rebounds
or 3 Rebounds

1. Start with a left jab by placing your left foot (same side as the jab hand) slightly in front of your right foot. Angle your shoulders so the left shoulder is slightly forward of your right one. Raise both hands just above shoulder level, making loose fists and pulling elbows together.

2. Strike out with your left fist, leaning slightly forward on your left foot and transferring your weight from your back foot to the end of your fist. Avoid twisting or leaning too far into this punch; hold your shoulders in the same position throughout. Visualize where your fist is going to land, which helps you throw the punch with confidence and authority. Turn your knuckles flat as they hit the bag.

3. Punch the bag with an even amount of power, then quickly bring your fist back to the starting position. Be ready to strike again. Count the rebounds as the bag moves forward and back. After five rebounds, jab again.

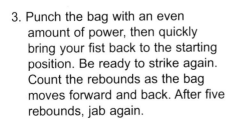

Basic Punches

Jab con't.

Right or Southpaw Jab

4. Switch sides by placing your right foot in front and leading with your right shoulder.

④

5. Strike with your right fist, leaning slightly forward on your right foot and transferring your weight from your back foot to the end of your fist. Avoid twisting or leaning too far into this punch; hold your shoulders in the same position throughout. Visualize where your fist is going to land, which helps you throw the punch with confidence and authority. Turn your knuckles flat as they hit the bag.

⑤

6. Hit the bag straight on so it rebounds forward and back in a straight motion. Let the bag rebound fives times before hitting it again.

⑥

Boxer's Box

The jab is the most important punch a boxer learns. Your jab measures the distance between you and your opponent. All the punch combinations you throw at an opponent are set up and timed off the jab. Some of the best boxers are known for their excellent jabs.

Cross

Cross: 5 Rebounds

1. Place your left foot (orthodox stance) slightly in front of your right foot. Angle your shoulders so the left shoulder is slightly forward of your right one. Raise both hands just above shoulder level, making loose fists and pulling elbows together.

2. Drop your left fist as you bring your right fist straight out, thrusting your right shoulder forward. Transfer your weight from your back foot to your front foot; twist your hips and shoulders to direct your fist to the target. Turn your shoulders and hips in the direction of the punch.

3. Hit the bag front and center, causing it to go straight and rebound at the front center of the board. Turn your knuckles to land flat against the bag.

Note: This punch is normally done in combination with a jab, also known as a 1-2 combination. The cross hand is opposite to the jabbing hand.

Basic Punches

Cross con't.

Left or Southpaw Cross

4. Switch sides; place your right foot in front and lead with your right shoulder.

④

5. Drop your right fist as you bring your left fist straight out, thrusting your left shoulder forward. Transfer your weight from your back foot to your front foot; twist your hips and shoulders to direct your fist to the target. Turn your shoulders and hips in the direction of the punch.

⑤

6. Hit the bag straight so it rebounds forward and back in a straight motion. Turn your knuckles to land flat against the bag.

⑥

Boxer's Box

The cross is commonly known as the power punch because you lean into it, putting your weight behind it. The power comes from transferring your weight off your back foot as you twist your hips and shoulders and extend your right arm and fist into the target.

Advanced
PUNCHES

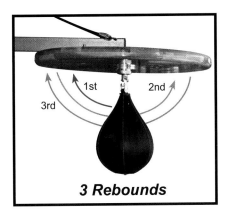

3 Rebounds

Three rebounds

Once you feel comfortable with five rebounds, take away one of the revolutions. So instead of counting to five, count three rebounds before hitting the bag again. This will improve your timing and coordination.

Continuous punching

Now that you know some basic punches, it's time to improve your rhythm, balance and timing by combining punches and using both hands. Everyone wants the bag to flow like music from the first punch. However, expecting this to happen without practice can lead to frustration. Start very slowly to get your timing correct and concentrate on hitting the bag in the direction you want it to go. Use the same amount of power each time.

Important: Make sure you are comfortable with only three rebounds of the bag with both the jab and the front forward strike before advancing your punches.

Front Circular Combination

Front Circular Combo:
3 Rebounds

1. Raise both fists together to the left side of your head, keeping your elbows at shoulder height.

2. Strike the bag with the outside of your left fist like with a front forward strike.

3. Hit the bag in the center so it travels straight forward and back.

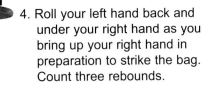

Front Circular Combination con't.

4. Roll your left hand back and under your right hand as you bring up your right hand in preparation to strike the bag. Count three rebounds.

④

5. After the third rebound, strike the bag with your right fist. The movements should be continuous, fluid and controlled.

⑤

6. Switch hands again, counting the rebounds and preparing to strike with your other hand. Use the same amount of power with both hands.

⑥

7. After a few minutes of continuous punching, stop and try again with your fists on the other side of your head.

⑦

Advanced Punches

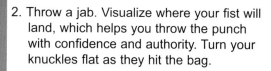

Jab-Cross

1. Start in the jab stance with your left hand and left foot in front of the right side of your body.

(1)

2. Throw a jab. Visualize where your fist will land, which helps you throw the punch with confidence and authority. Turn your knuckles flat as they hit the bag.

(2)

3. Punch directly forward and through the bag with an even amount of power, then quickly bring your fist back to the starting position. As you retract your jabbing fist, prepare to throw the cross punch.

(3)

Note: When you start putting punches together, the number of revolutions changes depending on which punch you throw. The jab always has three rebounds, and the cross always has five rebounds.

Jab-Cross con't.

4. Once the bag has rebounded three times and you return your jab hand to its starting position, push off your back foot, throwing a cross, nice and straight, with a little more power than the jab.

(4)

5. Visualize where your fist will land, which helps you throw the punch with confidence and authority. Turn your knuckles flat as they hit the bag.

(5)

6. Repeat the jab-cross combination. Throw your punches straight so the bag goes in the direction you want it to. Be consistent with the power you use for the jab and the cross. In other words, control the jab's power to rebound the bag three times and slightly increase the cross's power to rebound the bag five times; this keeps your rhythm.

(6)

Advanced Punches

Forward-Side

Start slowly; as you begin to feel more comfortable, increase the power of your punches, which speeds up the bag's revolutions.

Beginner

Front Forward Strike: 5 Rebounds
Side Strike: 5 Rebounds

Advanced

Front Forward Strike: 3 Rebounds
Side Strike: 3 Rebounds

1. Start in the orthodox boxer's stance, with your left foot and left fist forward.

2. Throw a front forward strike with your left hand.

3. Focus on hitting the bag directly in the center so it travels in a straight line.

Advanced Punches

Forward-Side con't.

4. After you hit the bag, let it rebound three times.

5. Immediately after your strike, circle your left fist back, placing it above your right eye.

6. Now strike the bag with the outside of your left fist by directing it toward the side of the bag.

Advanced Punches

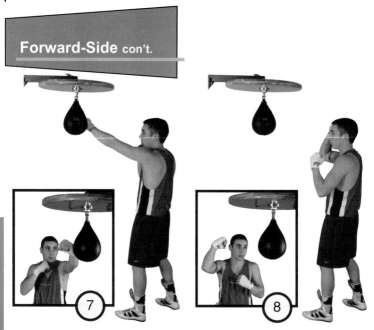

7 & 8. Hitting the bag from the left will cause it to travel
diagonally across the board. Switch hands; prepare to hit
the bag with your right hand using a front forward strike.

9 & 10. Contacting the bag will be more difficult because the
bag is not moving forward and back in a straight line. With
practice, you will find a nice rhythm.

11 & 12. After contacting the bag with a right front forward strike, circle your right fist back, placing it above your left eye.

13 & 14. Bringing your right fist across your face toward the left side of the bag, strike the side of the bag with the outside of your right fist. Continue; allowing three or five rebounds (depending on your skill level) between each hit.

SPEED BAG
DRILLS

Jab Drill

Jab: 3 Rebounds
Cross: 5 Rebounds

This drill is good for strengthening the boxer's most important punch: The jab. The drill helps improve your aim, timing, coordination and power.

1. Start in a boxing stance with your left hand and left foot slightly in front. Throw a jab at the bag, letting the bag rebound three times. Immediately throw a cross with enough power to make the bag rebound five times.

Left Jab
1 time

Right Cross
1 time

2. Now throw two jabs, one after the other, letting the bag rebound three times after each jab. After the second jab, throw a cross (after the bag has rebounded three times) with enough power to make the bag rebound five times.

Left Jab
2 times

Right Cross
1 time

2. Now throw two jabs, one after the other, letting the bag rebound three times after each jab. After the second jab, throw a cross (after the bag has rebounded three times) with enough power to make the bag rebound five times.

Left Jab
3 times

Right Cross
1 time

3. Increase the number of jabs to three in a row with three rebounds after each one. Follow the third jab with a right cross, allowing the bag to rebound five times after the cross.

4. Continue this drill until you reach 10 consecutive jabs. Reverse the sequence from 10 jabs back to one.

Switch Up

1. When you return to only one jab, switch sides and start the sequence with a right jab and a left cross.

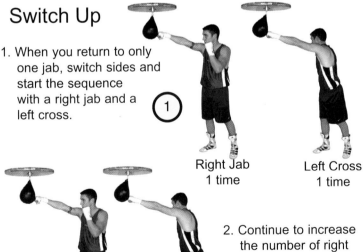

Right Jab
1 time

Left Cross
1 time

Right Jab
2 times

Left Cross
1 time

2. Continue to increase the number of right jabs until you reach 10; reverse the sequence from 10 jabs back to one.

Speed Bag Drills

Cross Drill

Jab: 3 Rebounds
Cross: 5 Rebounds

1. Start with your left hand and left foot slightly in front. Throw a jab, letting the bag rebound three times. Immediately throw a cross with enough power to make the bag rebound five times.

Left Jab 1 time   Right Cross 1 time

Left Jab 2 times   Right Cross 2 times

2. After five rebounds, throw a left jab, letting the bag rebound three times. Now throw another jab, letting the bag rebound three times again. Immediately throw a right cross with enough power to make the bag rebound five times. Throw a second cross, rebounding the bag five times.

3. Throw three consecutive jabs with three rebounds after each one. After the bag stops rebounding, throw three consecutive crosses with five rebounds after each one.

Left Jab 3 times   Right Cross 3 times

4. Continue this process until you reach 10 of each.

Speed Bag Drills

Cross Drill con't.

Switch Up

Repeat the same steps as on the previous page with the opposite hands. This drill helps improve coordination and timing.

1. Start with your right hand and right foot slightly in front. Throw a jab, letting the bag rebound three times. Immediately throw a left cross with enough power to make the bag rebound five times.

Right Jab 1 time   Left Cross 1 time

Right Jab 2 times   Left Cross 2 times

2. After the bag rebounds five times, throw a right jab, letting the bag rebound three times. Throw another jab, letting the bag rebound three times again. Immediately throw a left cross with enough power to make the bag rebound five times. Throw another cross, rebounding the bag five times.

Speed Bag Drills

3. Throw three consecutive jabs with three rebounds after each one. Throw three consecutive crosses with five rebounds after each one.

Left Jab 3 times   Left Cross 3 times

4. Continue this process until you reach 10 of each.

Twenty-Twenty

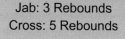

Jab: 3 Rebounds
Cross: 5 Rebounds

1. With your left foot forward, throw 20 consecutive left jabs, letting the bag rebound three times after each jab. When the bag has rebounded three times following the last jab, switch hands.

Left Jab
20 times

2. Now throw 10 consecutive right crosses, letting the bag rebound five times after each cross. When the bag has rebounded five times following the last cross, change your stance so the right foot is forward.

Right Cross
10 times

3. Throw 10 consecutive jabs with your right hand, letting the bag rebound three times after each one. You have now thrown 20 consecutive punches with your right hand.

Right Jab
10 times

4. Keep your stance the same, but switch hands again. Throw 10 consecutive left crosses, letting the bag rebound five times after each strike.

Left Cross
10 times

Speed Bag Drills

5. Change your stance again, placing your left foot forward. Throw 10 consecutive left jabs, allowing three rebounds after each strike. You have now thrown 20 consecutive punches with your left hand.

⑤

Left Jab 10 times

6. Now throw 10 consecutive right crosses, letting the bag rebound five times after each hit. After the last strike, change your stance so the right foot is forward.

⑥

Right Cross
10 times

7. Without changing hands, throw 10 consecutive right jabs, allowing the bag to rebound three times. You have now thrown 20 consecutive punches with your right hand.

⑦

Right Jab 10 times

8. Now throw 10 consecutive left crosses, letting the bag rebound five times after each one. After the last cross, change your stance so the left foot is forward.

⑧

Left Cross
10 times

9. Throw 10 consecutive left jabs, allowing the bag to rebound three times after each hit. You have now thrown 20 consecutive punches with your left hand.

⑨

Left Jab 10 times

Speed Bag Drills

Punch
ROUTINES

All of the following punch routines are based on 15 minutes each. Similar to an actual match in the ring with 3 minute segments of intense work and then a minute break.

Punch Routines

-3 MINUTES PUNCHING
-1 MINUTE BREAK
-3 MINUTES PUNCHING
-1 MINUTE BREAK
-3 MINUTES PUNCHING
-1 MINUTE BREAK
-3 MINUTES PUNCHING
15 MINUTE TOTAL ROUTINE

Punch Routine 1

Punch Routine 1

-3 MINUTES PUNCHING
-1 MINUTE BREAK
-3 MINUTES PUNCHING
-1 MINUTE BREAK
-3 MINUTES PUNCHING
-1 MINUTE BREAK
-3 MINUTES PUNCHING
15 MINUTE TOTAL ROUTINE

1. For 30 seconds, perform a front forward strike with your left hand, letting the bag rebound only three times after each strike.
2. Continue throwing left front forward strikes, one after the other, with the same amount of power and in the same direction.

Front Forward Strike with left hand for 30 seconds

Front Forward Strike (pg. 32)

3. After 30 seconds, change your stance and do a front forward strike with your right hand.
4. Try to switch your hands and your stance while the bag is moving.

Front Forward Strike with right hand for 30 seconds

Front Forward Strike (pg. 32)

Punch Routines

Punch
Routine 1 con't.

1. For 30 seconds, perform a front forward strike with your left hand, letting the bag rebound only three times after each strike.
2. Continue throwing left front forward strikes, one after the other, with the same amount of power and in the same direction.

Front Forward Strike with left hand for 30 seconds

Front Forward Strike (pg. 32)

3. After 30 seconds, change your stance and do a front forward strike with your right hand.
4. Try to switch your hands and your stance while the bag is moving.

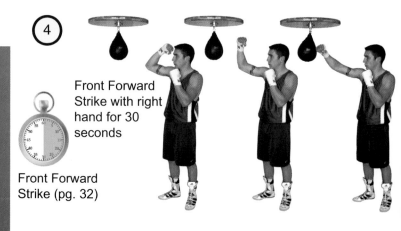

Front Forward Strike with right hand for 30 seconds

Front Forward Strike (pg. 32)

Punch Routines

**Punch
Routine 1 con't.**

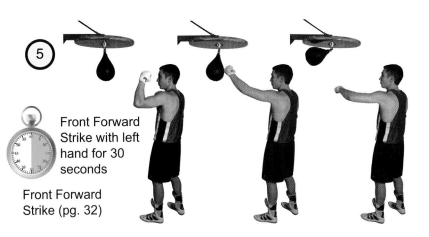

⑤

Front Forward
Strike with left
hand for 30
seconds

Front Forward
Strike (pg. 32)

5. Once you have thrown left front forward strikes for 30
   seconds, change your stance again; throw right front forward
   strikes for 30 seconds. Try to switch your hands and your
   stance while the bag is moving.

⑥

Front Forward
Strike with
right hand for
30 seconds

Front Forward
Strike (pg. 32)

Take a one-minute break; repeat the routine three times.

Punch Routine 2

1. For 30 seconds, throw straight left jabs with a good amount of power.
2. Let the bag rebound three times after each punch, then throw another jab.
3. Continue throwing left jabs, one after the other, with the same amount of power and in the same direction.
4. After 30 seconds, change your stance.
5. Try to switch your hands and your stance while the bag is moving.

Punch Routine 2

-3 MINUTES PUNCHING
-1 MINUTE BREAK
-3 MINUTES PUNCHING
-1 MINUTE BREAK
-3 MINUTES PUNCHING
-1 MINUTE BREAK
-3 MINUTES PUNCHING
15 MINUTE TOTAL ROUTINE

① Jab with left hand for 30 seconds

Jab (pg. 33)

② Jab with right hand for 30 seconds

Jab (pg. 33)

Punch Routines

**Punch
Routine 2 con't.**

6. After completing the right jabs, switch to throwing left front
   forward strikes for another 30 seconds.

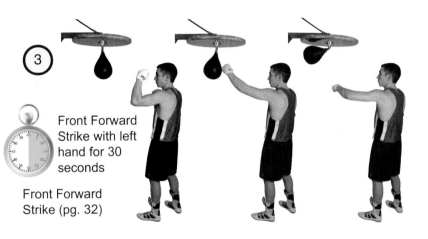

Front Forward
Strike with left
hand for 30
seconds

Front Forward
Strike (pg. 32)

7. Change your stance; throw right front forward strikes for 30
   seconds. Try to switch your hands and your stance while the
   bag is moving.

Front Forward
Strike with
right hand for
30 seconds

Front Forward
Strike (pg. 32)

Punch Routines

Punch
Routine 2 con't.

8. Now throw a front-forward-side combination with your left hand. Immediately follow that with a front-forward-side combination with your right hand.

Front Forward-Side with both hands for 60 seconds

Forward Side (pg. 42)

⑤

9. Continue throwing the front-forward-side combination, switching hands each time for the last minute of the segment.
10. Keep a steady pace during this three-minute segment.

Take a one-minute break; repeat the routine three times.

Punch
Routine 3

Punch Routine 3

-3 MINUTES PUNCHING
-1 MINUTE BREAK
-3 MINUTES PUNCHING
-1 MINUTE BREAK
-3 MINUTES PUNCHING
-1 MINUTE BREAK
-3 MINUTES PUNCHING
15 MINUTE TOTAL ROUTINE

1. Start with an orthodox position; throw a straight left jab with a good amount of power.
2. Let the bag rebound three times, then immediately throw another left jab.
3. Let the bag rebound three times, then immediately throw a right cross. Continue with this double-left-jab-right-cross combination for 30 seconds.

Left Jab-
Left Jab-
Right Cross
for 30
seconds

Jab (pg. 33)
Cross (pg. 35)

4. Change your stance; throw two right jabs followed by a left cross.
5. Try to switch your hands and your stance while the bag is moving.

Right Jab-
Right
Jab-Left
Cross for
30 seconds

Jab (pg. 33)
Cross (pg. 35)

Punch Routines

Punch
Routine 3 con't.

6. With both hands at your left eye-line, throw continuous front circular punches for 60 seconds.

③

Front Circular Punch for 60 seconds

Front Circular Punch (pg. 38)

7. After 60 seconds, prepare to finish the front-forward-side combination.

Punch Routines

Punch Routine 3 con't.

Front Forward-Side with both hands for 60 seconds

Forward Side (pg. 42)

8. Throw a front-forward-side combination with your left hand. Immediately follow that with a front-forward-side combination with your right hand.

9. Continue throwing the front-forward-side combination, switching hands each time for the last minute of the segment.
10. Keep a steady pace during this three-minute routine.

Take a one-minute break; repeat the routine three times.

Punch Routines

Other Products by
Productive Fitness Products Inc.

The Great Handbook Series

Canada $10.95   U.S. $8.95

The Great Handbook series are a wonderful addition to your exercise library. These books have all the different exercises you need for working your whole body. In addition, they discuss how to set up a program, how to stretch, how to stay motivated, and safety tips. All have 64 pages of exercises using popular pieces of fitness equipment. The books, sold separately, are written and edited by experts in a clear and concise manner, with step-by-step instructions and full color photos for all exercises.

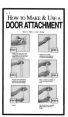

The Great Home Gym Handbook — The Quick Reference Guide to Home Gym Exercises

The Great Yoga Handbook — The Quick Reference Guide to Yoga Exercises

The Great Balance & Stability Handbook — The Quick Reference Guide to Balance & Stability Exercises

The Great Heavy Bag Handbook — The Quick Reference Guide to Heavy Bag use for boxing and kickboxing

The Great Speed Bag Handbook — The Quick Reference Guide to Speed Bag Exercises

The Ultimate Weight Training Journal

More than a <u>one-year personal fitness diary</u>, The Ultimate Weight Training Journal discusses basic nutrition, aerobics, and strength training. But best of all, this book shows you how these three tools can best be used in attaining a better physique, better health and more strength.

288 pages

One Year of Training Log pages based on 3-4 workouts per week.

Canada $18.95
U.S. $14.95

Body Ball Training Poster Pack
- Four Full-Color 12" x 18" Posters -

Four posters sold
as a set only

*Body Ball Training
Poster Pack*

<u>Laminated</u>

Canada $29.95
U.S. $22.95

• These four full-color, laminated posters will make your ball workouts more effective by allowing you to quickly identify proper exercise form and technique.

Dumbbell Training Poster Pack
- Four Full-Color 12" x 18" Posters -

Four posters sold
as a set only

*Dumbbell Training
Poster Pack*

<u>Laminated</u>

Canada $29.95
U.S. $22.95

• These four full-color, laminated posters will make your dumbbell workouts more effective by allowing you to quickly identify proper exercise form and technique.

Stretch Tubing Training Poster Pack
- Five Full-Color 12" x 18" Posters -

Five posters sold
as a set only

• These five full-color, laminated posters will make your stretch tubing workouts more effective by allowing you to quickly identify proper exercise form and technique.

*Stretch Tubing
Poster Pack*

<u>Laminated</u>

Canada $29.95
U.S. $22.95